Published by
Grandreams Limited,
Jadwin House, 205/211 Kentish Town Road,
London, NW5 2JU.

Printed in Czech Republic.

MY
FIRST
PICTURE
DICTIONARY

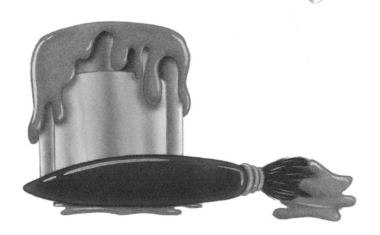

Addition

Finding how many things you have. 1+1=2

Alarm

A sound that is a signal. The alarm clock is ringing!

Alligator

A reptile very like a crocodile. They are found in lakes and rivers in the U.S.A. and China.

Anchor

A heavy-hooked piece of metal on a rope or chain that fastens a boat to the bottom of the sea or river bed.

Angry

When you are angry, you feel very cross about something. This boy is angry.

Ankle

The joint between your foot and leg. If you sprain your ankle, it hurts!

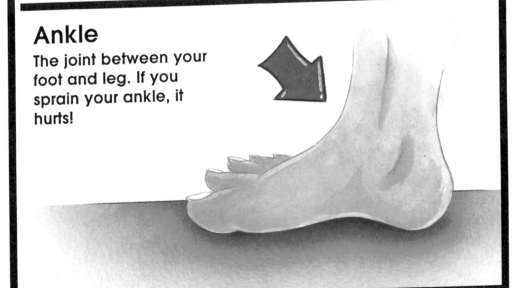

Apple

This fruit grows on a tree. You can eat apples raw, or cooked in an apple pie. Delicious!

Asleep

This boy is asleep. He is tired and resting. He is not awake.

Axe

A cutting tool with a wooden handle and sharp metal edge.

Bb

Badge
A little emblem worn on your clothes.

Balloon
Made of thin rubber, balloons float when you blow them up, because they fill with air.

Balls
Balls are round or oval. You can play games with a ball, you can catch, kick or throw it.

Bird

A bird is an animal covered in feathers, with wings and a tail. Most birds can fly. All baby birds are hatched from eggs.

Blackboard

A board painted black, you write on it with chalk.

Blue

On a clear sunny day, the sky is blue and so is the sea.

Bone

Bones make up your skeleton, which is the framework of your body. You have 206 bones.

Boots

Strong footwear that keep your feet and ankles dry and warm.

Box

You keep things in a box. The sides are straight and some boxes have lids.

Boy

This will be a man when he grows up. Now he is a young male child.

Bread

Bread is made from flour, water and yeast and baked in the oven.

Brick

Clay is baked into bricks to build walls and houses.

Brush

We use many different brushes, most have handles and bristles or hair.

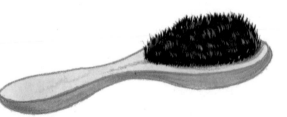

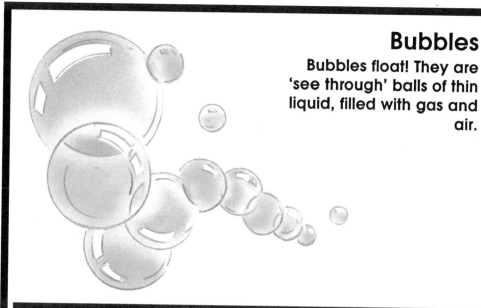

Bubbles

Bubbles float! They are 'see through' balls of thin liquid, filled with gas and air.

Burglar

If a burglar breaks into your home, he will steal things and take them away.

Butter

Cream is whipped until it turns into butter. You spread it on your toast.

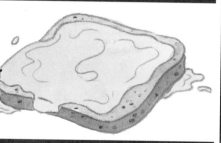

Button

Buttons are used to fasten clothes. They fit into a buttonhole.

Candle
Made of wax.
The wick burns
to give you light.

Cap
You wear a cap on your
head. Some boys wear a
cap to school.

Card
Cards send greetings! Did
you get many cards on your
birthday?

Carrot
A vegetable
with a long
tapering orange
root that grows
underground.

Cat

Cats are furry animals. We keep small cats at home as pets. They have long whiskers and often hunt and catch mice.

Caterpillar

A grub that will turn into a butterfly or a moth one day.

Chair

A chair is a seat for one. It is a piece of furniture to sit on. Some chairs are very comfortable.

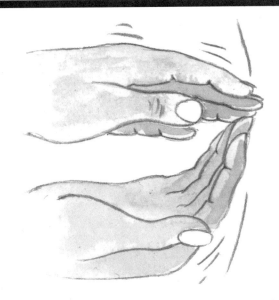

Clap

When you bring your hands together quickly and make a loud sound, you clap.

Cliffs

A sharp drop in the land. Don't go near a cliff edge!

Clock

We all tell the time by looking at the clock. It measures the minutes and hours in the day and during the night.

Clouds

Clouds in the sky are made of drops of water that fall as rain.

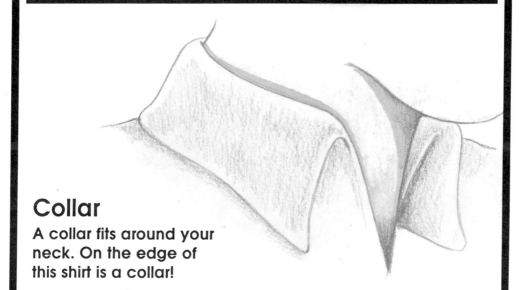

Collar

A collar fits around your neck. On the edge of this shirt is a collar!

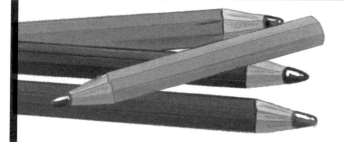

Crayons

You draw with coloured crayons, they are made of wax.

Cushion

A small soft pillow to sit on.

Daisy

A tiny white flower with a yellow centre.

Diamond

A sparkling precious stone, often made into jewellery.

Dice

You throw the dice to play board games, they are little cubes covered with dots.

Dinosaur

Gigantic animals that roamed the Earth millions of years ago. There are none left alive today!

Dog

People keep a dog as a pet. Guard dogs bark when visitors knock at the door.

Doll

Children love to play with a doll.
It is a small model of a person.

Dollar

Money used in the
U.S.A., Canada,
Australia, Singapore,
New Zealand and
Hong Kong.

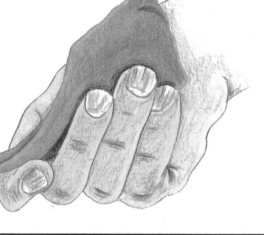

Dominoes

You play the game
dominoes with little
black oblong
pieces marked
with spots.

Donkey

An animal like a horse. It has long ears and makes a loud noise, 'Hee Haw'.

Door

The way in and out of a house, or room, is through the door.

Doughnut

A soft round cake, cooked in oil and rolled in sugar. Some have jam in the middle.

12

Dozen

A dozen is twelve and half a dozen is six.

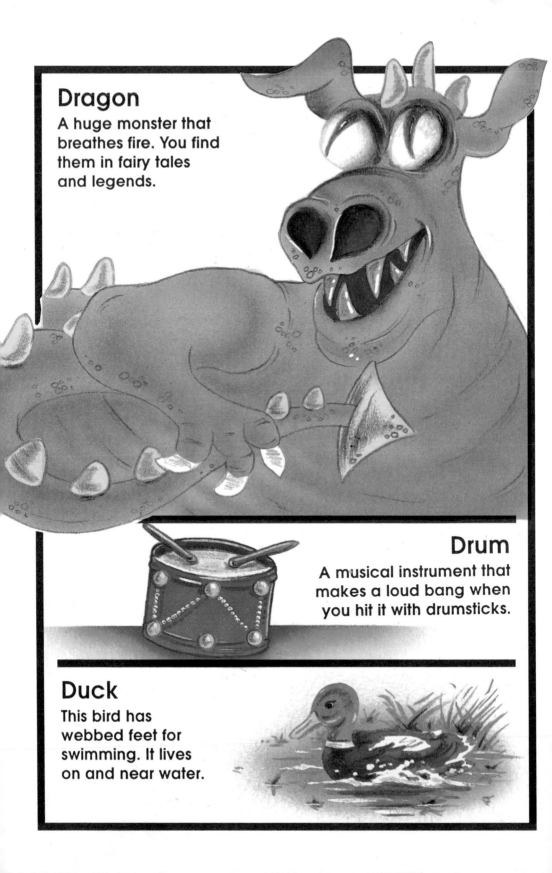

Dragon

A huge monster that breathes fire. You find them in fairy tales and legends.

Drum

A musical instrument that makes a loud bang when you hit it with drumsticks.

Duck

This bird has webbed feet for swimming. It lives on and near water.

Earth
The planet on which we live.

Egg
Birds lay eggs. The yellow part in the centre is the yolk.

Elephant
The largest animal that lives on land. Its long nose is called a trunk which is very useful for picking up things.

Eleven

Eleven comes after ten and before twelve. It is ten plus one.

Envelope

You put a letter in an envelope, stick a stamp on the front, write the address and post it!

Eraser

It rubs out something that has been written, perhaps a mistake!

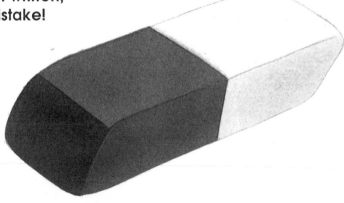

2 4 6 8

Even
All numbers that are even can be divided by two. 1, 3, 5, 7, are odd numbers.

Evening
When the light begins to fade, it is evening, the last part of the day.

Excellent
Excellent is very good, better than the rest!

Eyes
You see with your eyes. If you close them you will see nothing at all.

Ff

Face
Eyes, nose, cheeks, and chin are all parts of your face.

Fairy
These are tiny creatures from storybooks. Do you believe in fairies?

Family
All people who are related to you are your family.

Fence

It is a barrier built to keep things out, as well as keep things in. Do you climb over the garden fence?

Finger

At the end of each hand you have four fingers and one thumb.

Fire

When something burns, there are hot flames. Fire is very dangerous.

Fist

When you close your hand tightly into a ball.

5

Five

Five is the number before six and after four. 1+4=5.

Flag

A piece of cloth used as a sign. Every country has its own flag.

Flowers

Flowers are part of a plant, inside are the seeds. They attract insects and smell lovely.

Foot

You have a foot on the end of each leg. When you stand or walk, you put them on the ground.

Forest

Lots of trees growing together, a very large wood.

Fork

You use a fork to pick up your food.

Four

Four is an even number 2+2=4 and 1+3=4.

4

Fox

A reddish-brown wild animal that looks like a dog. It has a bushy tail and is very cunning.

Frog

A frog can live in water and on land. With its strong back legs, it can jump a long way.

Fruit

The seeds of a plant grow inside the fruit.

Gale

A very strong wind. Sometimes it can blow trees over.

Garden

A piece of land to grow flowers and vegetables. Playing in the garden can be fun.

Ghost

Ghosts are not real! Do you dress up for Halloween, pretend you are a ghost and give everyone a fright?

Giant

A giant is a huge person. You often read about them in fairy tales like 'Jack And The Giant Killer'.

Gift

A gift is a present. At Christmas and on birthdays, we give each other gifts.

Glasses

Glasses can help you to see and read better. Sunglasses shade our eyes from strong sunlight.

Gloves

Gloves cover your hands and keep them warm.

Goat

Goats are related to sheep. They give milk which makes cheese. Some goats have little beards!

Goose

A big heavy bird that can swim and fly, some farmers keep flocks of geese.

Green

Green is the colour of leaves in spring and summer. Grass is green too.

Grey

When a storm is coming the clouds in the sky are grey.

Grin

When you grin, your smile is very wide. Something is making you really happy.

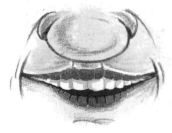

Hh

Hammer
A hammer is used to knock nails into place.

Hamster
A little furry animal with cheeks like pouches.

Handkerchief
You blow your nose on this small piece of cloth, or perhaps wipe a tear from your eye.

Hands

We use our hands to hold things. Friends shake hands when they meet.

Happy

When you are happy, you are very pleased and feel good about something.

Hat

You wear a hat on your head to keep it warm and dry. Shady hats keep off the hot sun.

Hay

Long grass, cut down, dried and used as food for animals.

Head

The part of your body above the neck, face at the front and hair on top.

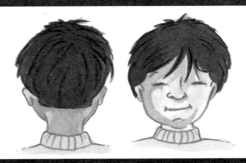

Heart

A red heart is sent to the one you love.

Heel

Your heel is the round part at the back of your foot.

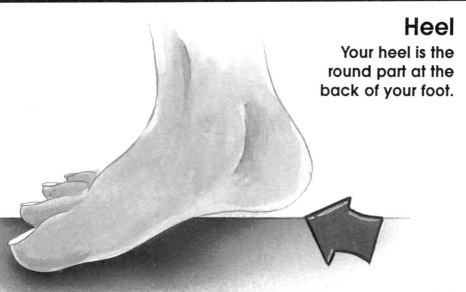

Hill

When you climb a hill, you are walking up a piece of high ground.

Hold

If you are holding something, you keep it in your hand.

Hole

A hole is an empty space in something, like a hole in a sock!

Hoof

The hand part of some animals' feet. Cows and horses have hooves.

Hook

A hook is a bent piece of metal to catch hold of things.

Horns

Some animals have horns. Cattle have horns on their heads, but a rhinoceros has a horn on its nose.

Huge

Something that is very large. The elephant is huge, but a mouse is tiny.

100

Hundred

Ten times ten is one hundred. A century is one hundred years.

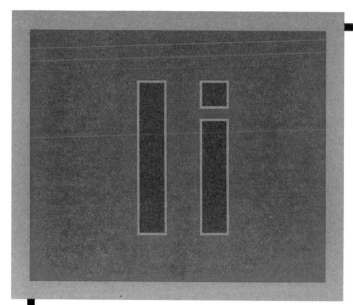

Ice
Ice is frozen water, cold, solid and hard.

Ice cream
A frozen dessert made with cream and sugar. It comes in lots of delicious flavours.

Ice skates
Strong boots mounted on blades for moving across the ice. Can you skate?

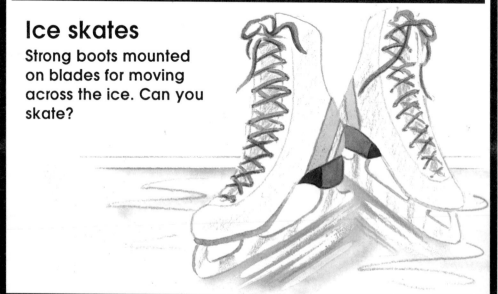

Igloo

A house built of frozen snow blocks. Eskimos find them very warm inside.

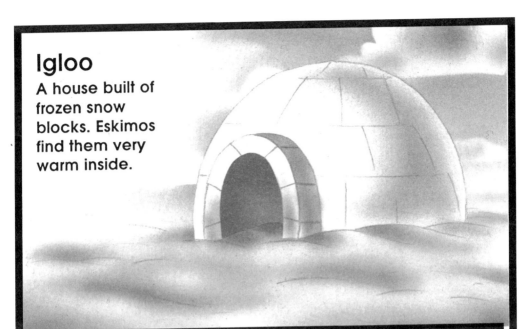

Ink

When you write, your pen is full of a coloured liquid called ink.

Island

A piece of land with water all the way around. Australia is a huge island.

Jj

Jar
Jars have lids and often hold food.

Jeans
Trousers made from strong cloth called denim.

Jelly
When it is set, jelly is clear and wobbly. It is made from fruit juice and gelatine.

Jigsaw

A picture puzzle cut into pieces. You must fit them back together.

Jug

It is easy to pour liquids from a jug, it has a small spout on its rim.

Jumper

You pull a jumper over your head and wear it on chilly days. They are often made of wool.

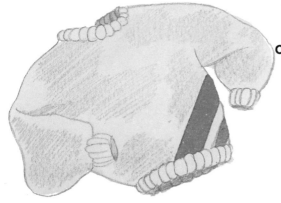

Kk

Kangaroo

It carries its baby in a pouch at the front!

Kennel

If you want to keep a dog outside, you put it in its own little house called a kennel.

Key

It fits into a keyhole to lock and unlock things. Keys unlock and start a car!

King

A king rules his country. He often wears a crown and lives in a palace.

Kite

Made of cloth or paper on a frame. A kite flies high in the air when the wind blows.

Kitten

A young cat is called a kitten. They are very mischievous and love to play with a ball of wool.

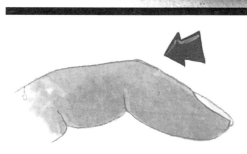

Knuckle

Small joints that make your fingers bend.

Label

It tells you about something, or what is inside.

Ladle

A deep spoon for lifting out liquids, soup perhaps! It has a curved handle.

Ladybird

A familiar little red beetle with black spots. It has six legs and can fly.

Lamb

Lambs are young sheep. They are soft and woolly and are born in early spring.

Lamp

Lamps give us light inside the house or outside on a tall lamppost.

Leaves

Leaves cover trees and plants. Some trees loose their leaves in the autumn.

Legs

Legs support your body. On two legs you can walk, run, jump and kick.

Lemon

A juicy, yellow fruit that tastes sour. Add water and sugar to lemon juice and you have lemonade!

Leopard

This fierce wild animal is like a large cat. It has yellowish-brown fur with black spots.

Letter

A letter is a written message. You post a letter in a letter box.

Lettuce

A crisp green vegetable used in salads. Caterpillars love lettuce!

Lightning

During a storm, you see the flash of lightning in the sky before you hear the thunder.

Lips

Lips are two thin rims around your mouth. You can smile with your lips. Some girls paint their lips with red lipstick!

Lizard

A scaly, cold blooded reptile. Some have long tongues and tails. They like warm dry places.

Lollipops

Frozen fruit juice. A frozen drink on a lollipop stick, lovely on a hot day.

Magnet
They pull
metal objects
towards them.

Marbles
Little coloured glass
balls. Children use them
to play the game of
marbles.

Match
A small wooden stick that
catches fire when you rub
it along the side of a
matchbox. Do not play
with matches!

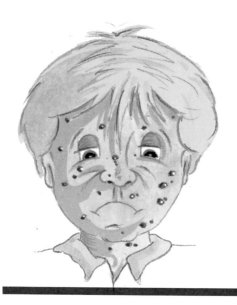

Measles
If you catch measles, your body and face is covered in tiny red spots. No school until you get better!

Meat
Part of an animal we eat as food. Beef comes from cattle, pork from pigs.

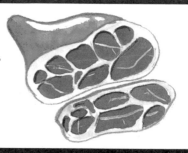

Mermaid
Mermaids are sea creatures that appear in fairy tales and fables.

Milk
We drink milk and use it to make butter and cheese. It comes from cows and goats.

Miser

A miser keeps money and never likes to spend it. Mr. Scrooge in 'A Christmas Carol' was a miser.

Mole

A small, dark, furry animal that burrows underground and throws up small mounds of earth.

Moon

As the moon spins round the Earth, the Sun's light catches the surface of the moon and shines.

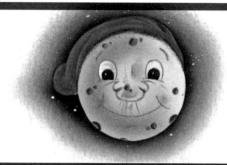

Mountain
A very high hill with steep rocky sides. Some mountains are so high, they have snow on top.

Mushroom
You can eat some mushrooms, but others are poisonous. Do not pick them!

Music
Music is the sound made by instruments. When you sing, you make music with your voice.

Nn

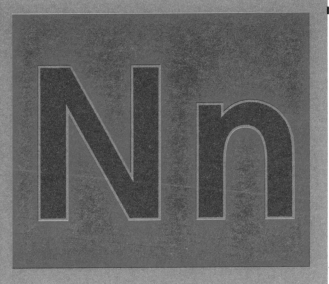

Nail
A thin piece of metal with a sharp point.

Napkin
A square cloth of soft paper to keep your clothes clean at meal times.

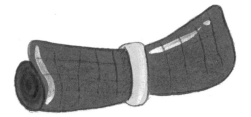

Neck
It joins your head to your body wear a neckloc neck.

Newspaper

Thin printed sheets of paper that tell you all the latest happenings around the world.

9 Nine

Number nine comes after eight and before ten. 3 x 3 = 9.

Nose

Your nose is used for breathing, sneezing and smelling. It is in the middle of your face.

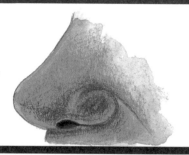

Nuts

Inside the hard shell of a nut, you will find a seed. Some are good to eat!

O'Clock

When we tell the time by the clock, we say something o'clock.

1

One

One means a single thing. There is only one, just on its own.

Onion

This vegetable smells and tastes strongly. If you peel an onion it will make your eyes run and tears stream down your face.

Orange

A round, sweet juicy fruit, orange in colour. Do you like freshly squeezed orange juice?

Otter

Otters live in burrows along river banks. They have webbed toes and are good swimmers.

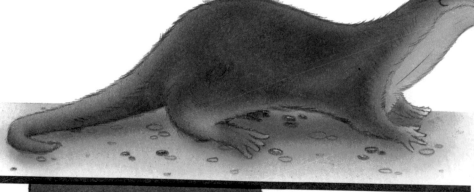

Oven

Food is cooked in a hot oven. In it, you can roast and bake.

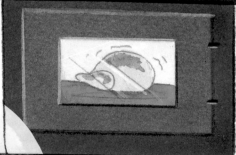

Overalls

Garments worn over your clothes to keep them clean. Motor mechanics always wear overalls.

Owl

A bird with wide eyes, sharp claws and a hooked beak. Owls hunt at night and hoot.

Pp

Pail

A bucket with a handle to hold liquids.

Paint

Paint is a coloured liquid put on with a paintbrush. Dad painted the door red!

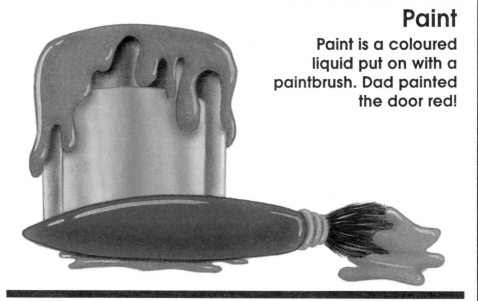

Parcel

A parcel is something wrapped up in paper. The postman often delivers them.

Parrot

These birds have brightly coloured feathers, and sharp hooked beaks which they use to crack nuts and seeds.

Patch

A patch over your eye looks like a little shield. Pirates often wore eye-patches.

Pea

Peas are small, round green vegetables that grow side by side in a pod.

Peach

A sweet juicy fruit with a velvety skin and large stone in the centre.

Pear

A juicy fruit that grows on a tree. It is round at the bottom and grows narrower towards the stalk.

Pen

You can write with a pen, it is filled with ink.

Pencil

A thin, wooden stick to write with. It has a black or coloured middle.

Pets

Tame animals that you love and look after.

Photograph

Photographs are pictures taken with a camera that has a film inside.

Picture

A picture is a drawing, a painting or photograph of almost anything.

Pie

Meat or fruit baked inside a pastry crust. Delicious!

Pillow

A cushion to rest your head on when you go to sleep.

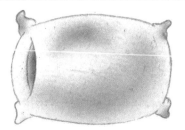

Pineapple

A sweet yellowish fruit that grows in hot countries. It is shaped like a pine cone.

Pirate

Robbers on the high seas that stole from ships long ago.

Plum

Plums can be purple, yellow, green or red. This fruit makes wonderful pies!

Pocket

A little bag stitched inside a dress, trousers or jacket.

Point

When you point, you stick your finger out to show which way. It's rude to point at someone!

Polo neck

A high fitting collar on a sweater that can be turned over at the top.

Pond

A pool of water smaller than a lake, it often contains wildlife.

Potatoes

Round lumpy vegetables that grow underground.

Pumpkin

This vegetable can grow to an enormous size. Here is a Halloween pumpkin.

Puppies

Puppies are very young dogs. They are lovable little creatures.

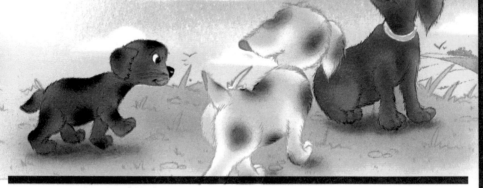

Puzzle

A puzzle makes you think. It is often difficult to solve.

Quarter
A quarter is one of
four equal pieces.

Queen
A woman who rules her country. Her
husband is a king or a prince.

Question mark
When you write a sentence that
asks a question, you end it with a
question mark. Don't you?

Rr

Rabbit
A furry animal that lives in a burrow underground.

Racing car
A car built to go very fast on a special race track.

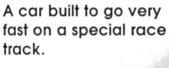

Radio
Radios receive then play sound waves that come through the air.

Rain

Tiny water droplets that
fall from the sky onto
the earth below.

Rainbow

A rainbow is split up into seven different colours. It
happens when the sun shines through raindrops.

Raspberry

A small bright red fruit, very
like a blackberry. They are
often made into jam.

Rattle

A baby's toy. When you shake it,
you can hear a rattling sound.

Read

When you read a book, you look at the words and understand them.

Record

You put a record on a record player when you want to listen to music. It is a round piece of plastic with a hole in the middle.

Red

Red is the colour of blood. Red is for danger. It is bright and easy to see.

Ribbon
A long narrow band of coloured material.

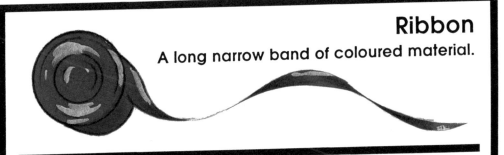

Right
A right answer is correct. It is not wrong.

Ripped
When something is torn open, it is ripped.

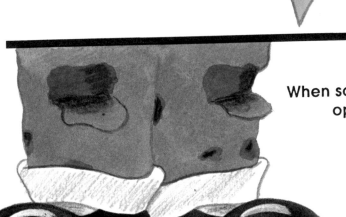

Road
The road takes people from place to place, watch the road for traffic!

Rock

A large piece of hard stone. Mountains are made from rock.

Roll

Shaped like a small loaf of bread, just big enough for one person to eat.

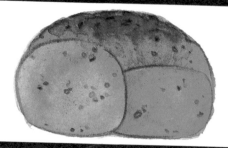

Rolling pin

When you want to make pastry, you roll it flat with a rolling pin.

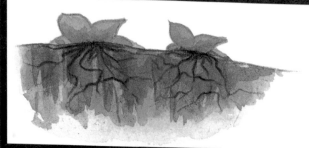

Roots

Part of the plant that grows down into the ground and takes in food and water.

Rope

A rope is a thick strong twisted cord made up of lots of thin cords.

Rose

A beautiful flower grown in gardens and hedges. Some have sharp thorns that can prick your finger.

Rubber

You use a rubber to rub out pencil marks.

Ss

Sack
A large bag for holding things.

Sail
When you sail, you take a trip on a ship. A sail catches the wind and makes the boat go fast.

C3OLI

Sandcastle
You build a sandcastle on the beach with a bucket and spade and lots of sand.

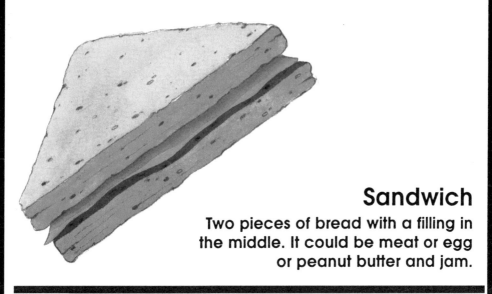

Sandwich

Two pieces of bread with a filling in the middle. It could be meat or egg or peanut butter and jam.

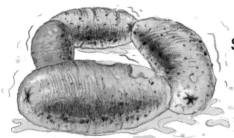

Sausages

Sausages sizzling in a pan are made from minced meat stuffed into a skin.

Scissors

A pair of scissors has two sharp blades fixed in the middle. You cut things with them.

Sea

Sea covers two thirds of the earth. The water in the sea is salty.

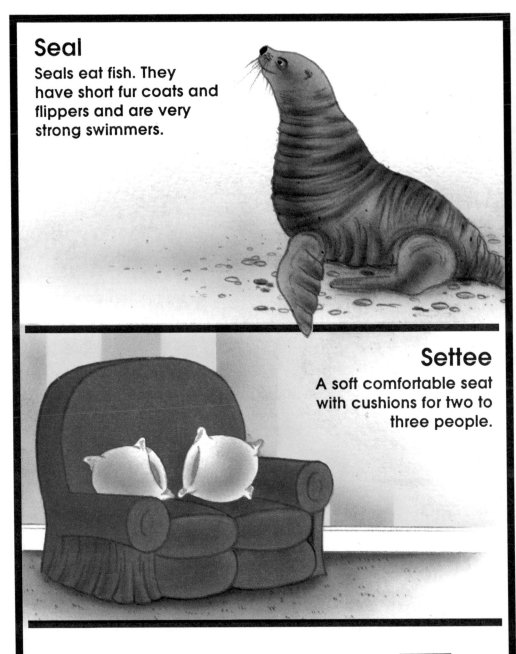

Seal

Seals eat fish. They have short fur coats and flippers and are very strong swimmers.

Settee

A soft comfortable seat with cushions for two to three people.

Seven

Seven comes after six but before eight. There are seven days in a week.

7

Shapes

Everything has a shape. A circle is a round shape.

Shoes

We wear shoes to keep our feet warm and dry.

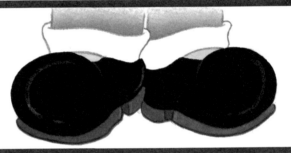

Shorts

Shorts are trousers that come above the knee. Do you wear shorts for sport?

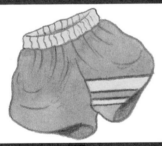

Shout

To speak very loudly is to shout. Do not shout in class.

Signs

A sign is a notice that tells you something. Road signs help drivers.

6 Six

Six is after five but before seven.
$3 \times 2 = 6$.

Skirt

Girls wear skirts. It is a piece of clothing that hangs from the waist, and is often worn with a blouse.

Skull

Your skull is at the top of your spine. Your brain is inside this hard bony case. Pirates fly the skull and crossbones flag!

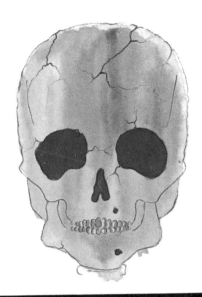

Sky

If you go outside and look up, the sky is above you.

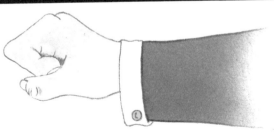

Sleeve

The sleeve of your coat or sweater covers your arm.

Slippers

A soft comfortable pair of indoor shoes, they slip on easily.

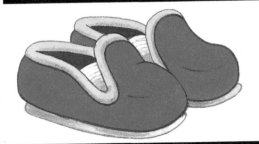

Smile

When you are happy or pleased, you turn up the corners of your mouth and smile.

Smoke

When you see or smell smoke, something is on fire.

Snakes

Snakes shed their skin from time to time. Some are poisonous and are very dangerous.

Snowman

When the snow is thick, children build a snowman and dress him in a hat and scarf.

Soap

We wash ourselves with soap and water and the dirt disappears.

Socks

You wear socks on your feet inside your shoes to keep your feet warm.

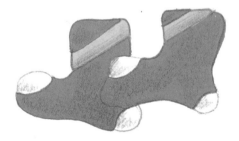

Spoon

You eat and stir things with a spoon.

Stars

Stars are very far away
in space. You can see
them twinkling in the
sky at night.

Strawberry

A bright red soft fruit with a
green stalk on top.
Strawberries and cream are
a treat!

Sums

When you add or subtract numbers, you are finding their
total or sum.

$$2 + 4 = 6$$
$$6 - 4 = 2$$

Sun

The sun gives us light and heat. It is a ball of burning gases millions of miles away from Earth.

Sweat

When you sweat, tiny drops of moisture appear on your skin. It is the body's way of keeping cool.

Sword

A weapon with a long blade with sharp edges for stabbing and cutting.

Tacks
Sharp nails with round flat heads.

Tambourine
A musical instrument like a narrow drum. You can tap it or wave it in the air with one hand.

Teddy bear
A soft cuddly furry toy, loved by children and grown-ups all over the world.

Television

A television gives us pictures and sounds from signals sent from far away. We receive them through an aerial.

10 Ten

Ten is the number after nine.
10 x 10 = 100.

Toes

At the end of each foot you have five toes. Two feet, ten toes!

Tomato

The tomato is a fruit, often grown in greenhouses. We eat it raw in salads. It is made into soups and sauces and tomato ketchup.

Tongue

Part of your mouth which helps to taste and talk.

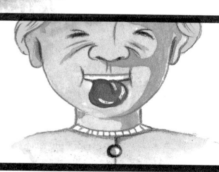

Tools

You need tools to help you work and make things.

Tooth

All animals, including us, need teeth to bite and chew food.

Tortoise

A slow moving reptile with a bony hard shell on its back. They hibernate in cold weather.

Towel

A soft fluffy piece of cloth, used to dry yourself when you've had a bath or shower.

Trap door

A door in the floor
sometimes on stage.
People vanish through a
trap door.

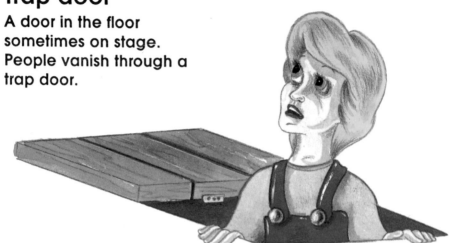

Tree

A tree is the largest kind of
plant. Branches grow from
the trunk and the roots
spread underground.

Triangle

A shape with three
straight sides.

Trousers

Trousers cover the legs.
They are fastened at the
waist by a belt.

Ugly
Not very good-looking.

Umbrella
You hold an umbrella over your head to keep you dry when it is raining. It looks like a walking stick when it is closed up.

Unhappy
Here is an unhappy boy. He is crying and looks sad.

Valentine
A sweetheart chosen on 14th February.

Valley
The lower ground that lies between hills or mountains.

Vase
A vase is a container for flowers. Make sure it is filled with water, or the flowers will die.

Vegetables

Vegetables are plants grown for food. We can eat them cooked or raw.

Vest

A vest keeps you warm, worn underneath a shirt or blouse.

Volcano

A mound that throws out red hot liquid rock, gases and ash when it erupts.

Wafer
A thin crispy biscuit, often served with ice cream.

Wall
A wall is a boundary built of brick or stone, on the side of a house.

Walrus
A large sea mammal that lives in the Arctic. It has long tusks and a bristly moustache.

Warm

When you feel warm, you are not hot and you are not cold, just in-between.

White

When there is no colour on the paper it is white. As white as snow!

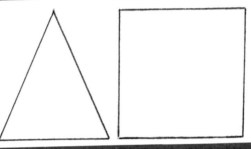

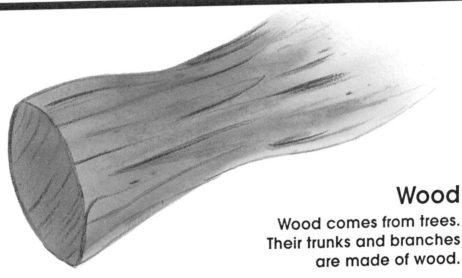

Wood

Wood comes from trees. Their trunks and branches are made of wood.

World

Everything around us is the world. The whole earth and sky is the world we live in.

Worm

Worms are very long and thin with no legs. They burrow down into the earth where they live in enormous numbers.

Wrist

Your wrist joins your hand to your arm. Bend your wrist and move your hand.

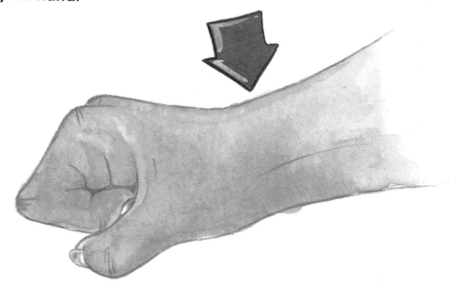

Wrong

If you do something you shouldn't, it is wrong! Wrong is opposite to right.

X

X is the sign that means multiply.
3 x 3 = 9

X-ray

A special kind of photograph that shows the inside of your body. Broken bones are X-rayed.

Xylophone

You hit little blocks of wood or metal with hammers to play a tune.

Yy

Yacht
A small boat with sails.

Yawn
When you are tired or bored, you open your mouth wide and yawn. You make other people yawn too!

Yellow
A bright sunny colour. Bananas, daffodils and lemons are all yellow.

Zebra

A wild horse with black and white stripes.

Zig-zag

A line painted on a road that has sharp corners and bends.

Zip

A zip has two sets of teeth that grip together. Some clothes and bags have zips.